T0025297

THE BOOK OF
GREATEST
LEADERSHIP
QUOTATIONS

THE BOOK OF
GREATEST
LEADERSHIP
QUOTATIONS

▲▲

AN INSPIRING COLLECTION ON CREATIVITY, TEAMWORK, & EMPOWERMENT

THE BOOK OF GREATEST LEADERSHIP QUOTATIONS

Text Copyright © 2022 Hatherleigh Press

Library of Congress Cataloging-in-Publication Data is available.
ISBN: 978-1-57826-885-6

Printed in the United States
10 9 8 7 6 5 4 3 2 1

"He who has never learned to obey
cannot be a good commander."

—ARISTOTLE

CONTENTS

INTRODUCTION

When we're confronted with the unknown or unexpected, it can feel as though we've wandered into a dark cave with no exit. It is at these times that we turn to leaders, those who can hold a flashlight in front of us, helping us find our way out.

Be it in the business world, in sports or civic engagement, impactful leadership provides the context and vision necessary for bringing groups of people together to take bold, innovative next steps. Our most talented leaders are those who can see the potential in a person that he or she might not realize is there. They coax out the best version of ourselves. Through their belief in us, we learn more, strive to do better, and become inspired to develop our own leadership potential.

The quotes in this collection include wisdom from CEOs, generals, coaches and legislators. They define moments that are emblematic of inspired leadership. The ability to envision the growth possibility for a team, a company, a movement, or a nation is a key identifying trait of a great leader. Enduring personal sacrifice and having the confidence and conscience to stand alone is another. A leader's willingness to roll up his or her sleeves and share the burden in service to the group and their shared cause also factors in.

The collective knowledge and experience of the great individuals gathered within this collection span centuries. Draw inspiration from them when you're called upon to play a leadership role for those around you.

CREATING THE CULTURE

Leaders create the kind of organizational culture that allows it to succeed. The strongest leaders in the business world are those who can create an atmosphere that supports innovation while nurturing a sense of community and shared purpose among their staff.

START WITH GOOD PEOPLE, LAY OUT the rules, communicate with your employees, motivate them and reward them. If you do all those things effectively, you can't miss.

—LEE IACOCCA

A LEADER'S JOB IS TO LOOK INTO THE future and see the organization, not as it is, but as it should be.

—JACK WELCH

THERE IS A DIFFERENCE BETWEEN being a leader and being a boss. Both are based on authority. A boss demands blind obedience; a leader earns his authority through understanding and trust.

—KLAUS BALKENHOL

COMING TOGETHER IS A BEGINNING; keeping together is progress; working together is success.

—HENRY FORD

IF ONE IS LUCKY, A SOLITARY FANtasy can totally transform one million realities.

—MAYA ANGELOU

TOO MANY COMPANIES BELIEVE people are interchangeable. Truly gifted people never are. They have unique talents. Such people cannot be forced into roles they are not suited for, nor should they be. Effective leaders allow great people to do the work they were born to do.

—WARREN BENNIS

AS A LEADER, I AM TOUGH ON MYSELF and I raise the standard for everybody; however I am very caring because I want people to excel at what they are doing so that they can aspire to be me in the future.

—INDRA NOOYI

INTERDEPENDENT PEOPLE COMBINE their own efforts with the efforts of others to achieve their greatest success.

—STEPHEN COVEY

TRUST IS THE LUBRICATION THAT makes it possible for organizations to work.

—WARREN BENNIS

YOUR FIRST AND FOREMOST JOB AS a leader is to take charge of your own energy and then help to orchestrate the energy of those around you.

—PETER F. DRUCKER

LEADERS MUST ENCOURAGE THEIR organizations to dance to forms of music yet to be heard.

—WARREN BENNIS

LEADERSHIP IS THE ART OF GETTING someone else to do something you want done because he wants to do it.

—DWIGHT D. EISENHOWER

IF EVERYTHING SEEMS UNDER CON-
trol, you're not going fast enough.

—MARIO ANDRETTI

MANAGEMENT IS DOING THINGS
right; leadership is doing the right things.

—PETER F. DRUCKER

LEADERSHIP IS UNDERSTANDING
people and involving them to help you do a
job. That takes all of the good characteristics,
like integrity, dedication of purpose, selflessness,
knowledge, skill, implacability, as well as deter-
mination not to accept failure.

—ARLEIGH BURKE

THINK OF YOURSELF AS AN ATHLETE. I guarantee you it will change the way you walk, the way you work, and the decisions you make about leadership, teamwork, and success.

—MARIAH BURTON NELSON

YOU HAVE TO LEAD PEOPLE GENTLY toward what they already know is right.

—PHIL CROSBY

IF YOU WANT TO BUILD A SHIP, DON'T drum up the men to gather wood, divide the work, and give orders. Instead, teach them to yearn for the vast and endless sea.

—ANTOINE DE SAINT-EXUPÉRY

AN ORGANIZATION, NO MATTER HOW well designed, is only as good as the people who live and work in it.

—DEE HOCK

A GENUINE LEADER IS NOT A searcher for consensus but a molder of consensus.

—MARTIN LUTHER KING, JR.

MY OWN DEFINITION OF LEADERSHIP is this: the capacity and the will to rally men and women to a common purpose and the character which inspires confidence.

—BERNARD LAW MONTGOMERY

IF YOU'RE TRYING TO CREATE A company, it's like baking a cake. You have to have all the ingredients in the right proportion.

—ELON MUSK

IF YOUR ACTIONS CREATE A LEGACY that inspires others to dream more, learn more, do more and become more, then, you are an excellent leader.

—DOLLY PARTON

THE LEADERS WHO WORK MOST effectively, it seems to me, never say "I." They don't think "I." They think "we"; they think "team."

—TOM PETERS

MANAGEMENT IS ABOUT ARRANGING and telling. Leadership is about nurturing and enhancing.

—TOM PETERS

THE GREATEST LEADER IS NOT NEC-essarily the one who does the greatest things. He is the one that gets the people to do the greatest things.

—RONALD REAGAN

EXAMPLE IS NOT THE MAIN THING in influencing others. It is the only thing.

—ALBERT SCHWEITZER

A LEADER IS A DEALER IN HOPE.

—NAPOLEON BONAPARTE

THE LEADER SEES LEADERSHIP AS responsibility, rather than as rank and privilege.

—PETER DRUCKER

LEADERSHIP IS NOT ABOUT A TITLE or a designation. It's about impact, influence and inspiration. Impact involves getting results, influence is about spreading the passion you have for your work, and you have to inspire team-mates and customers.

—ROBIN S. SHARMA

IF YOU WOULD CONVINCE A MAN that he does wrong, do right. Men will believe what they see.

—HENRY DAVID THOREAU

LEADERSHIP IS BASED ON INSPIRA-tion, not domination; on cooperation, not intimidation.

—WILLIAM ARTHUR WARD

AN ORGANIZATION'S ABILITY TO learn, and translate that learning into action rapidly, is the ultimate competitive advantage.

—JACK WELCH

SUCCESS OR FAILURE IN BUSINESS IS caused more by the mental attitude even than by mental capacities.

—WALTER SCOTT

THE LEADER IS ONE WHO MOBILIZES others toward a goal shared by leader and followers.

—GARRY WILLS

YOU CAN'T LIVE A PERFECT DAY without doing something for someone who will never be able to repay you.

—JOHN WOODEN

I KNOW OF NO SINGLE FORMULA FOR success. But over the years I have observed that some attributes of leadership are universal and are often about finding ways of encouraging people to combine their efforts, their talents, their insights, their enthusiasm and their inspiration to work together.

—QUEEN ELIZABETH II

IN ORGANIZATIONS, REAL POWER and energy is generated through relationships. The patterns of relationships and the capacities to form them are more important than tasks, functions, roles, and positions.

—MARGARET J. WHEATLEY

MOTIVATION COMES FROM WORKING on things we care about. It also comes from working with people we care about.

—SHERYL SANDBERG

THE KEYS TO SUCCESS ARE PATIENCE, persistence, and obsessive attention to detail.

—JEFF BEZOS

EMPOWERING THOSE AROUND YOU

The best leaders help their charges see character traits and abilities in themselves they didn't know existed. Their passion and empathy builds the foundation for future success in those around them.

OUR CHIEF WANT IS SOMEONE WHO will inspire us to be what we know we could be.

—RALPH WALDO EMERSON

THE TASK OF LEADERSHIP IS NOT TO put greatness into people, but to elicit it, for the greatness is there already.

—JOHN BUCHAN

IF YOUR ACTIONS INSPIRE OTHERS to dream more, learn more, do more, and become more, you are a leader.

—JOHN QUINCY ADAMS

A GOOD OBJECTIVE OF LEADERSHIP is to help those who are doing poorly to do well and to help those who are doing well to do even better.

—JIM ROHN

LEADERSHIP IS NOT MAGNETIC personality that can just as well be a glib tongue. It is not "making friends and influencing people"—that is flattery. Leadership is lifting a person's vision to high sights, the raising of a person's performance to a higher standard, the building of a personality beyond its normal limitations.

—PETER F. DRUCKER

As we look ahead into the next century, leaders will be those who empower others.

—BILL GATES

The real leader has no need to lead—he is content to point the way.

—HENRY MILLER

Everyone has an invisible sign hanging from their neck saying, "Make me feel important." Never forget this message when working with people.

—MARY KAY ASH

A LEADER TAKES PEOPLE WHERE they want to go. A great leader takes people where they don't necessarily want to go, but ought to be.

—ROSALYNN CARTER

THE MEDIOCRE TEACHER TELLS. The good teacher explains. The superior teacher demonstrates. The great teacher inspires.

—WILLIAM ARTHUR WARD

THE GROWTH AND DEVELOPMENT of people is the highest calling of leadership.

—HARVEY S. FIRESTONE

AS FOR THE BEST LEADERS, THE people do not notice their existence. [...] When the best leader's work is done the people say, "We did it ourselves!"

—LAO TZU

LEADERSHIP IS THE ABILITY TO guide others without force into a direction or decision that leaves them still feeling empowered and accomplished.

—LISA CASH HANSON

NO MAN WILL MAKE A GREAT LEADER who wants to do it all himself or get all the credit for doing it.

—ANDREW CARNEGIE

LEADERSHIP IS UNLOCKING PEOPLE'S potential to become better.

—BILL BRADLEY

HUMANS ARE AMBITIOUS AND rational and proud. And we don't fall in line with people who don't respect us and who we don't believe have our best interests at heart. We are willing to follow leaders, but only to the extent that we believe they call on our best, not our worst.

—RACHEL MADDOW

THE KEY TO SUCCESSFUL LEADERSHIP is influence, not authority.

—KENNETH H. BLANCHARD

LEADERS MUST BE CLOSE ENOUGH to relate to others, but far enough ahead to motivate them.

—JOHN C. MAXWELL

PEOPLE WHO ARE TRULY STRONG lift others up. People who are truly powerful bring others together.

—MICHELLE OBAMA

BEFORE YOU ARE A LEADER, SUCCESS is all about growing yourself. When you become a leader, success is all about growing others.

—JACK WELCH

ULTIMATELY, LEADERSHIP IS NOT about glorious crowning acts. It's about keeping your team focused on a goal and motivated to do their best to achieve it, especially when the stakes are high and the consequences really matter. It is about laying the groundwork for others' success, and then standing back and letting them shine.

—CHRIS HADFIELD

A LEADER IS LIKE A SHEPHERD. HE stays behind the flock, letting the most nimble go out ahead, whereupon the others follow, not realizing that all along they are being directed from behind.

—NELSON MANDELA

OUTSTANDING LEADERS GO OUT OF their way to boost the self-esteem of their personnel. If people believe in themselves, it's amazing what they can accomplish.

—SAM WALTON

THE FUNCTION OF LEADERSHIP IS TO produce more leaders, not more followers.

—RALPH NADER

THE GOAL OF MANY LEADERS IS TO get people to think more highly of the leader. The goal of a great leader is to help people to think more highly of themselves.

—J. CARLA NORTCUTT

DON'T TELL PEOPLE HOW TO DO things. Tell them what to do and let them surprise you with their results.

—GEORGE S. PATTON

AS A LEADER YOU SHOULD ALWAYS start with where people are before you try to take them to where you want them to go.

—JIM ROHN

THE BEST LEADER IS THE ONE WHO has sense enough to pick good men to do what he wants done, and the self-restraint to keep from meddling with them while they do it.

—THEODORE ROOSEVELT

I WAS NEVER THE SMARTEST GUY IN the room. From the first person I hired, I was never the smartest guy in the room. And that's a big deal. And if you're going to be a leader—if you're a leader and you're the smartest guy in the world—in the room, you've got real problems.

—JACK WELCH

KEEP YOUR FEARS TO YOURSELF, BUT share your courage with others.

—ROBERT LOUIS STEVENSON

I'LL LIFT YOU AND YOU'LL LIFT ME and we'll both ascend together.

—JOHN GREENLEAF WHITTIER

A LEADER IS THE MAN WHO HAS THE
ability to get other people to do what they don't
want to do, and like it.

—HARRY S. TRUMAN

AVERAGE LEADERS RAISE THE BAR
on themselves; good leaders raise the bar for
others; great leaders inspire others to raise their
own bar.

—ORRIN WOODWARD

A STAR WANTS TO SEE HIMSELF RISE
to the top. A leader wants to see those around
him rise to the top.

—SIMON SINEK

LEADERSHIP ON THE FIELD

Long-term growth and achievement are never the result of one person. Strong leaders know they need to have the right team around them to get the job done. The most admired sports heroes and coaches are those who inspire teammates and players to give all they were capable of and leave it on the field.

LEADERSHIP IS DIVING FOR A LOOSE ball, getting the crowd involved, getting other players involved. It's being able to take it as well as dish it out. That's the only way you're going to get respect from the players.

—LARRY BIRD

ONE MAN CAN BE A CRUCIAL INGREDient on a team, but one man cannot make a team.

—KAREEM ABDUL-JABBAR

I DON'T LOOK AT MYSELF AS A BASketball coach. I look at myself as a leader who happens to coach basketball.

—MIKE KRZYZEWSKI

TEAM PLAYER: ONCE WHO UNITES others toward a shared destiny through sharing information and ideas, empowering others and developing trust.

—DENNIS F. KINLAW

A LOT OF LEADERS FAIL BECAUSE they don't have the bravery to touch that nerve or strike that chord. Throughout my years, I haven't had that fear.

—KOBE BRYANT

WINNING ISN'T EVERYTHING, BUT the will to win is everything.

—VINCE LOMBARDI

THE STRENGTH OF THE TEAM IS each individual member. The strength of each member is the team.

—PHIL JACKSON

TREAT A PERSON AS HE IS, AND HE will remain as he is. Treat him as he could be, and he will become what he should be.

—JIMMY JOHNSON

INDIVIDUAL COMMITMENT TO A group effort—that is what makes a team work, a company work, a society work, a civilization work.

—VINCE LOMBARDI

LEADERSHIP IS GETTING PLAYERS to believe in you. If you tell a teammate you're ready to play as tough as you're able to, you'd better go out there and do it. Players will see right through a phony. And they can tell when you're not giving it all you've got.

—LARRY BIRD

EARN YOUR LEADERSHIP EVERY DAY.

—MICHAEL JORDAN

A LEADER HAS TO BE POSITIVE about all things that happen to his team. Look at nothing in the past as failure.

—MIKE KRZYZEWSKI

LEADERSHIP IS A MATTER OF HAVING people look at you and gain confidence, seeing how you react. If you're in control, they're in control.

—TOM LANDRY

THE GREAT LEADERS ARE LIKE THE best conductors—they reach beyond the notes to reach the magic in the players.

—BLAINE LEE

LEADERSHIP, LIKE COACHING, IS fighting for the hearts and souls of men and getting them to believe in you.

—EDDIE ROBINSON

LEADERS AREN'T BORN, THEY ARE made. And they are made just like anything else, through hard work. And that's the price we'll have to pay to achieve that goal, or any goal.

—VINCE LOMBARDI

TALENT WINS GAMES, BUT TEAM-work and intelligence wins championships.

—MICHAEL JORDAN

DURING CRITICAL PERIODS, A leader is not allowed to feel sorry for himself, to be down, to be angry, or to be weak. Leaders must beat back these emotions.

—MIKE KRZYZEWSKI

THE STRENGTH OF THE GROUP IS the strength of the leaders.

—VINCE LOMBARDI

EVERY LEADER NEEDS TO REMEMBER that a healthy respect for authority takes time to develop. It's like building trust. You don't instantly have trust, it has to be earned.

—MIKE KRZYZEWSKI

SOME PEOPLE WANT IT TO HAPPEN, some wish it would happen, others make it happen.

—MICHAEL JORDAN

A LEADER'S JOB IS TO DEVELOP COMmitted followers. Bad leaders destroy their followers' sense of commitment.

—DEAN SMITH

A PLAYER WHO MAKES A TEAM great is better than a great player.

—JOHN WOODEN

WHEN A LEADER TAKES RESPONSIbility for his own actions and mistakes, he not only sets a good example, he shows a healthy respect for people on his team.

—MIKE KRZYZEWSKI

THE MOST IMPORTANT THING IN good leadership is truly caring.

—DEAN SMITH

NOTHING WILL WORK UNLESS YOU DO.

—JOHN WOODEN

THE WAY A TEAM PLAYS AS A WHOLE determines its success. You may have the greatest bunch of individual stars in the world, but if they don't play together, the club won't be worth a dime.

—BABE RUTH

THERE'S NO WAY AROUND HARD
work. Embrace it.

—ROGER FEDERER

LEADERSHIP IS MORE ABOUT WHAT
you do, not what you say.

—DEREK JETER

LEADERSHIP UNDER FIRE

The most precarious moments in history pivoted on political courage and leadership on the battlefield. We look to our generals, presidents and civil rights heroes to inspire us to step up and take bold action during challenging times.

A TRUE LEADER HAS THE CONFI-dence to stand alone, the courage to make tough decisions, and the compassion to listen to the needs of others. He does not set out to be a leader, but becomes one by the equality of his actions and the integrity of his intent.

—DOUGLAS MACARTHUR

LEADERSHIP IS SOLVING PROBLEMS. The day soldiers stop bringing you their problems is the day you have stopped leading them. They have either lost confidence that you can help or concluded you do not care. Either case is a failure of leadership.

—COLIN POWELL

MOUNTAINTOPS INSPIRE LEADERS, but valleys mature them.

—WINSTON CHURCHILL

MEN MAKE HISTORY AND NOT THE other way around. In periods where there is no leadership, society stands still. Progress occurs when courageous, skillful leaders seize the opportunity to change things for the better.

—HARRY S. TRUMAN

WHEN PLACED IN COMMAND, TAKE charge.

—NORMAN SCHWARZKOPF

IN MATTERS OF STYLE, SWIM WITH the current; in matters of principle, stand like a rock.

—THOMAS JEFFERSON

THE ULTIMATE MEASURE OF A MAN is not where he stands in moments of comfort and convenience, but where he stands at times of challenge and controversy.

—MARTIN LUTHER KING, JR.

A LEADER DOES NOT DESERVE THE name unless he is willing occasionally to stand alone.

—HENRY KISSINGER

THE TRULY GREAT LEADER OVER-comes all difficulties, and campaigns and battles are nothing but a long series of difficulties to be overcome. The lack of equipment, the lack of food, the lack of this or that are only excuses; the real leader displays his quality in his triumphs over adversity, however great it may be.

—GEORGE C. MARSHALL

A LEADER IS A MAN WHO CAN ADAPT principles to circumstances.

—GEORGE S. PATTON

LEADERS GRASP NETTLES.

—DAVID OGILVY

TIME IS NEUTRAL AND DOES NOT change things. With courage and initiative, leaders change things.

—JESSE JACKSON

A CHIEF IS A MAN WHO ASSUMES responsibility. He says, "I was beaten," he does not say, "My men were beaten."

—ANTOINE DE SAINT-EXUPÉRY

THE SUPREME QUALITY FOR LEADership is unquestionably integrity. Without it, no real success is possible, no matter whether it is on a section gang, a football field, in an army, or in an office.

—DWIGHT D. EISENHOWER

DON'T EVER LET UP. DON'T EVER think that your job is unimportant. Every man has a job to do and he must do it. Every man is a vital link in the great chain.

—GEORGE S. PATTON

I HAVE ALWAYS SUPPORTED MEA-sures and principles and not men.

—DAVY CROCKETT

THE MOST IMPORTANT THING I learned is that soldiers watch what their leaders do. You can give them classes and lecture them forever, but it is your personal example they will follow.

—COLIN POWELL

THE TASK OF THE LEADER IS TO GET his people from where they are to where they have not been.

—HENRY KISSINGER

IT IS BETTER TO LEAD FROM BEHIND and to put others in front, especially when you celebrate victory when nice things occur. You take the front line when there is danger. Then people will appreciate your leadership.

—NELSON MANDELA

YOU DON'T LEAD BY HITTING PEOPLE over the head—that's assault, not leadership.

—DWIGHT D. EISENHOWER

WHAT WE NEED FOR LEADERS ARE men of the heart who are so helpful that they, in effect, do away with the need of their jobs. But leaders like that are never out of a job, never out of followers. Strange as it sounds, great leaders gain authority by giving it away.

—JAMES STOCKDALE

LEADERSHIP AND LEARNING ARE indispensable to each other.

—JOHN F. KENNEDY

ALWAYS DO EVERYTHING YOU ASK of those you command.

—GEORGE S. PATTON

A LEADER WHO DOESN'T HESITATE before he sends his nation into battle is not fit to be a leader.

—GOLDA MEIR

IT IS AMAZING WHAT YOU CAN accomplish if you do not care who gets the credit.

—HARRY S. TRUMAN

THE FINAL TEST OF A LEADER IS that he leaves behind him in other men the conviction and the will to carry on.

—WALTER LIPPMANN

EFFECTIVE LEADERS ARE MADE, NOT born. They learn from trial and error, and from experience.

—COLIN POWELL

LEADERSHIP—LEADERSHIP IS ABOUT taking responsibility, not making excuses.

—MITT ROMNEY

LEADERSHIP IS A POTENT COMBINA- tion of strategy and character. But if you must be without one, be without the strategy.

—NORMAN SCHWARZKOPF

HE WHO HAS NEVER LEARNED TO obey cannot be a good commander.

—ARISTOTLE

WHEN I AM GETTING READY TO reason with a man, I spend one-third of my time thinking about myself and what I am going to say and two-thirds about him and what he is going to say.

—ABRAHAM LINCOLN

I AM NOT AFRAID OF AN ARMY OF lions led by a sheep; I am afraid of an army of sheep led by a lion.

—ALEXANDER THE GREAT

A LEADER IS ONE WHO, OUT OF MAD-
ness or goodness, volunteers to take upon himself
the woe of the people. There are few men so
foolish, hence the erratic quality of leadership
in the world.

—JOHN UPDIKE

GREAT LEADERS ARE ALMOST ALWAYS
great simplifiers, who can cut through argument,
debate, and doubt to offer a solution everybody
can understand.

—COLIN POWELL

LEADERSHIP IS ABSOLUTELY ABOUT
inspiring action, but it is also about guarding
against mis-action.

—SIMON SINEK

You learn far more from negative leadership than from positive leadership. Because you learn how not to do it. And, therefore, you learn how to do it.

—NORMAN SCHWARZKOPF

HUMBLE LEADERSHIP

The most influential leaders are often those who can build consensus within the group. They achieve this unity by showing themselves as servants of the cause, which works to draw people together. Acts of service to the group and the cause are ultimately what move the wheels of progress forward.

TO LEAD PEOPLE, WALK BESIDE THEM.

—LAO TZU

THE BEST LEADERS ARE CLEAR. THEY continually light the way, and in the process, let each person know that what they do makes a difference. The best test as a leader is: Do those served grow as persons; do they become healthier, wiser, freer, more autonomous, more likely themselves to become leaders?

—ROBERT K. GREENLEAF

HUMILITY IS A GREAT QUALITY OF leadership which derives respect and not just fear or hatred.

—YOUSEF MUNAYYER

THE GREATNESS OF A MAN IS NOT in how much wealth he acquires but in his integrity and in his ability to affect those around him positively.

—BOB MARLEY

WE MUST BE SILENT BEFORE WE CAN listen. We must listen before we can learn. We must learn before we can prepare. We must prepare before we can serve. We must serve before we can lead.

—WILLIAM ARTHUR WARD

SERVING OTHERS PREPARES YOU TO lead others.

—JIM GEORGE

LEADERSHIP SHOULD BE BORN OUT of the understanding of the needs of those who would be affected by it.

—MARIAN ANDERSON

THE HIGHEST REWARD FOR A PERson's toil is not what they get for it, but what they become by it.

—JOHN RUSKIN

IT'S NOT ABOUT TRYING TO FIND something to help you be a more effective leader. It's about trying to be a better person. The other will follow.

—JAMES A. AUTRY

SERVANT LEADERSHIP IS ALL ABOUT making the goals clear and then rolling your sleeves up and doing whatever it takes to help people win. In that situation, they don't work for you; you work for them.

—KENNETH H. BLANCHARD

WE MAKE A LIVING BY WHAT WE GET. We make a life by what we give.

—WINSTON CHURCHILL

YOUR REWARDS IN LIFE WILL BE IN direct proportion to the value of your service to others.

—BRIAN TRACY

THE SIGNS OF OUTSTANDING LEAD-
ership appear primarily among the followers.
Are the followers reaching their potential? Are
they learning? Serving? Do they achieve the
required results? Do they change with grace?
Manage conflict?

—MAX DE PREE

TO COMMAND IS TO SERVE, NOTHING
more and nothing less.

—ANDRE MALRAUX

A NOBLE LEADER ANSWERS NOT TO
the trumpet calls of self-promotion, but to the
hushed whispers of necessity.

—MOLLIE MARTI

SERVANT-LEADERSHIP IS MORE than a concept, it is a fact. Any great leader, by which I also mean an ethical leader of any group, will see herself or himself as a servant of that group and will act accordingly.

—M. SCOTT PECK

THE EAR OF THE LEADER MUST RING with the voices of the people.

—WOODROW WILSON

SERVANT LEADERSHIP ALWAYS EMPA-thizes, always accepts the person, but sometimes refuses to accept some of the person's effort or performance as good enough.

—ROBERT K. GREENLEAF

LEADERSHIP IS ABOUT MAKING OTHers better as a result of your presence and making sure that impact lasts in your absence.

—SHERYL SANBERG

EGO CAN'T SLEEP. IT MICROMANages. It disempowers. It reduces our capability. It excels in control.

—ROBERT K. GREENLEAF

NOBODY CARES HOW MUCH YOU know, until they know how much you care.

—THEODORE ROOSEVELT

IF YOU WANT TO LIFT YOURSELF UP,
lift up someone else.

—BOOKER T. WASHINGTON

BE GENTLE AND YOU CAN BE BOLD;
be frugal and you can be liberal; avoid putting
yourself before others and you can become a
leader among men.

—LAO TZU

THE LED MUST NOT BE COMPELLED;
they must be able to choose their own leader.

—ALBERT EINSTEIN

A LEADER IS BEST WHEN PEOPLE barely know that he exists.

—WITTER BYNNER

THE FIRST RESPONSIBILITY OF A leader is to define reality. The last is to say thank you. In between, the leader is a servant.

—MAX DE PREE

ORGANIZATIONS EXIST TO SERVE. Period. Leaders live to serve. Period.

—TOM PETERS

HUMILITY IS THE SOLID FOUNDA-
tion of all virtues.

—CONFUCIUS

DO YOU WISH TO RISE? BEGIN BY
descending. You plan a tower that will pierce
the clouds? Lay first the foundation of humility.

—SAINT AUGUSTINE

DEVELOPING YOUR LEADERSHIP POTENTIAL

No one is born a leader. Leadership skills develop with experience, coaching, and hard work. To fully develop your leadership potential, you must observe the techniques and strategy of the successful influencers in your life. Study the character traits and follow the examples of modern and historical leaders.

THE MOST DANGEROUS LEADERSHIP myth is that leaders are born—that there is a genetic factor to leadership. This myth asserts that people simply either have certain charismatic qualities or not. That's nonsense; in fact, the opposite is true. Leaders are made rather than born.

—WARREN BENNIS

THE ART OF LEADERSHIP IS SAYING no, not saying yes. It is very easy to say yes.

—TONY BLAIR

LEADERSHIP IS A CHOICE, NOT A position.

—STEPHEN COVEY

MOST PEOPLE WHO WANT TO GET ahead do it backward. They think, "I'll get a bigger job, then I'll learn how to be a leader." But showing leadership skill is how you get the bigger job in the first place. Leadership isn't a position, it's a process.

—JOHN C. MAXWELL

THE PESSIMIST COMPLAINS ABOUT the wind; the optimist expects it to change; the realist adjusts the sails.

—WILLIAM ARTHUR WARD

IF A WINDOW OF OPPORTUNITY appears, don't pull down the shade.

—TOM PETERS

GREAT LEADERS ARE NOT DEFINED by the absence of weakness, but rather by the presence of clear strengths.

—JOHN PETER ZENGER

EVERYONE WHO'S EVER TAKEN A shower has an idea. It's the person who gets out of the shower, dries off and does something about it who makes a difference.

—NOLAN BUSHNELL

A MAN WHO WANTS TO LEAD THE orchestra must turn his back on the crowd.

—MAX LUCADO

ENLIGHTENED LEADERSHIP IS SPIR-
itual if we understand spirituality not as some kind
of religious dogma or ideology but as the domain
of awareness where we experience values like truth,
goodness, beauty, love and compassion, and also
intuition, creativity, insight and focused attention.

—DEEPAK CHOPRA

DON'T FIND FAULT, FIND A REMEDY.

—HENRY FORD

LEADERS LIVE BY CHOICE, NOT BY
accident.

—MARK GORMAN

LEADERS ARE FASCINATED BY future. You are a leader if and only if, you are restless for change, impatient for progress and deeply dissatisfied with status quo. Because in your head, you can see a better future. The friction between 'what is' and 'what could be' burns you, stirs you up, propels you. This is leadership.

—MARCUS BUCKINGHAM

WE CANNOT BECOME WHAT WE NEED by remaining what we are.

—JOHN C. MAXWELL

EVERY TIME YOU HAVE TO SPEAK, you are auditioning for leadership.

—JAMES HUMES

SOMETIMES WHEN YOU INNOVATE, you make mistakes. It is best to admit them quickly, and get on with improving your other innovations.

—STEVE JOBS

IF THE LEADER IS FILLED WITH HIGH ambition and if he pursues his aims with audacity and strength of will, he will reach them in spite of all obstacles.

—CARL VON CLAUSEWITZ

EFFECTIVE LEADERSHIP IS NOT about making speeches or being liked; leadership is defined by results not attributes.

—PETER F. DRUCKER

WHEN EVERYTHING SEEMS TO BE going against you, remember that the airplane takes off against the wind, not with it.

—HENRY FORD

A GOOD LEADER TAKES A LITTLE more than his share of the blame, a little less than his share of the credit.

—ARNOLD H. GLASOW

THE VERY ESSENCE OF LEADERSHIP is that you have to have vision. You can't blow an uncertain trumpet.

—THEODORE HESBURGH

LEADERSHIP IS A WAY OF THINKING, a way of acting and, most importantly, a way of communicating.

—SIMON SINEK

BECOME THE KIND OF LEADER THAT people would follow voluntarily; even if you had no title or position.

—BRIAN TRACY

NOTHING SO CONCLUSIVELY PROVES a man's ability to lead others as what he does from day to day to lead himself.

—THOMAS J. WATSON

JUST AS DISCIPLINE AND FREEDOM are opposing forces that must be balanced, leadership requires finding the equilibrium in the dichotomy of many seemingly contradictory qualities between one extreme and another.

—JOCKO WILLINK

EFFECTIVE LEADERSHIP IS PUTTING first things first. Effective management is discipline, carrying it out.

—STEPHEN COVEY

LEADERSHIP CONSISTS NOT IN degrees of technique but in traits of character.

—LEWIS H. LAPHAM

THE CHALLENGE OF LEADERSHIP IS to be strong but not rude; be kind, but not weak; be bold, but not a bully; be humble, but not timid; be proud, but not arrogant; have humor, but without folly.

—JIM ROHN

LEADERS THINK AND TALK ABOUT the solutions. Followers think and talk about the problems.

—BRIAN TRACY

A LEADER IS ONE WHO KNOWS THE way, goes the way, and shows the way.

—JOHN C. MAXWELL

THE LEADER HAS TO BE PRACTICAL and a realist, yet must talk the language of the visionary and the idealist.

—ERIC HOFFER

YOU CAN MOTIVATE BY FEAR, AND you can motivate by reward. But both those methods are only temporary. The only lasting thing is self-motivation.

—HOMER RICE

THE MAN WHO WILL USE HIS SKILL and constructive imagination to see how much he can give for a dollar, instead of how little he can give for a dollar, is bound to succeed.

—HENRY FORD

ONE OF THE BEST PARADOXES OF leadership is a leader's need to be both stubborn and open-minded. A leader must insist on sticking to the vision and stay on course to the destination. But he must be open-minded during the process.

—SIMON SINEK

IF YOU CAN'T SWALLOW YOUR PRIDE, you can't lead. Even the highest mountain had animals that step on it.

—JACK WEATHERFORD

PEOPLE BUY INTO THE LEADER before they buy into the vision.

—JOHN C. MAXWELL

LEADERSHIP IS THE SUM OF THOSE qualities of intellect, human understanding, and moral character that enables a person to inspire and control a group of people successfully.

—JOHN A. LEJEUNE

CONCLUSION

Leadership is needed in moments big and small, from organizing a family around a project on the house or steering a project at work forward to bringing a team to a championship or directing an army on the battlefield.

No large-scale task or collective effort can successfully come together without leadership. It is our leaders who drive us toward what is possible for the group and for ourselves. The vision and focus of strong leaders is needed in all avenues of life.

Refer back to the quotes in this collection whenever you feel the need to steel your resolve and find inspiration from the leadership challenges presented to you. Put aside any doubts about your own potential or abilities as a leader. Leadership skills develop from a willingness to learn and grow in service of a larger purpose. To that end, the wisdom of these business, military, civil, and sports leaders are tools to help you continue in your development as a leader.